plastic

Also by Matthew Rice

The Last Weather Observer

plastic

A Poem

Matthew Rice

 soft skull
new york

plastic

First Soft Skull edition: 2026

Library of Congress Cataloging-in-Publication Data
Names: Rice, Matthew, 1980- author
Title: Plastic : a poem / Matthew Rice.
Description: First Soft Skull edition | New York : Soft Skull, 2026. |
    Includes bibliographical references.
Identifiers: LCCN 2025034810 | ISBN 9781593768034 trade
    paperback | ISBN 9781593768041 ebook
Subjects: LCGFT: Poetry
Classification: LCC PR6118.I355 P57 2026 | DDC 821/.92—dc23/
    eng/20250801
LC record available at https://lccn.loc.gov/2025034810

Cover design by Victoria Maxfield
Cover image © iStock / Tim Parker
Book design by Laura Berry

Soft Skull Press
New York, NY
www.softskull.com

Printed in the United States of America

10 9 8 7 6 5 4 3 2 1

. . . the question of maintaining or transgressing the barrier that separates those who think from those who work with their hands.

Contents

plastic

Just as accidents wait
for boredom,
as illness waits
for health,

as comfort waits
for unemployment,
and salary cuts for wealth,
so may I, driven

to the industrial gate,
look for the treasure
buried
in my father's field.

I wake at 3 a.m., the hour no one
wants. Really, it's my heart that wakes me
beating its way out.
I pace the floor and sing under my breath
the song of the calm
and wonder if the factory is doing this.
It's Monday tomorrow, it always is when dreams are alarms.

How twenty-first century

the factory we pull ourselves out of bed for
the cliffs inside us crumbling into the ocean,
nozzles purging old material for moulded births,
frequent-flying formaldehyde greeting our lungs
the clock-in machine says thank you thank you
thank you to our fingerprint;
our grateful fifteen minutes at ten o'clock
the fresh air of a cigarette.

Bobby the Spark parallels the hours ahead
with a marathon, not a sprint, to be countered
with an ultramarathon, not a marathon,
as the weekly wage puts us back in the black;
we see it out till eight, the day shift finish at five,
laying down their dustpans and brushes, emptying the bins.

I shave my hair to suede,
I Mary Celeste,

    I facial hair,
    I sleeves rolled, I
    uniform,
    I mirror,
                I boots loose,
                I steel-toe,
                I mask up,
                I drive,
    I clock in,
      I throw down,
    I tool up,
      I obey,
                  I skive,
                      I resent,

                I burden
                I oil up

    I drill press,
    I scrub down,
    I sit,
    I stand

I lie, I lie,

I outlast,
        I barely last.

[Night shift]

Always on the drive to the factory I visit
somewhere I've never been, Amsterdam
sometimes, a gust of gulls sown
over the Singelgracht; or to Ronda maybe,
another timeline where the matadors

for good lay down their muletas.
The car park's uninsured Novas
slumber like peccadilloes and amid
night's tranquil abuse confectionaries of light
mean the moon to us sleepless

for the sake of the sleeping – this strange
hour this strange roost some fowls flutter
into, whose word you'd take
as you would a diamond.

19:57

The French horn of the snail
in the car park is equal

to the aperture of the wind
and silent as a bell.

Though no winter breath halos
above its head,

its pumpenvalve trail
glistens a path beyond the dead.

20:00

Abbots Cross Primary, rain-driven commutes,
butterflies in the back of a Talbot Sunbeam,
all becoming one with the promise of ordinary things.

The '80s have been and gone leaving only my disdain
for the factory radio blaring
Tina Turner's 'The Best'.

Once, in this building, a kid clocked off night shift
for good at the end of a rope,
another's heart gave out at 3 a.m.

performing a task as menial as mine.
I think
of the Rue de Seine,

ne travaillez jamais

       eroding into the wall.

20:01

It's been fifteen years

since he arrived
with a few empty phrases

to work through the night,
a shaft of morning sun

warming his fleece
when, near the big machine,

they found him hanging
at the first klaxon.

20:03

Bagging and tagging

plastic table latches
for aeroplane seats

my hands are each its twin
and my copy of *Gawain*

is contraband beneath
the frosted-out skylight

all a-tinkle
with rain coming down

as rain must
to make itself heard

but the factory will never glisten
as it glistens this evening

when out of nowhere,
at the industrial park entrance,

two hares are each its twin.

20:23

During the job interview
when I uttered my own name,

the awareness of self,
as if I hadn't earned the vowels,

rang strange in my head,
hung in the office

like necessity or myth:
Rice, from the Welsh, *Rhys*, descended

from the last true king of Wales.

20:29

The dappling light and all its implications
are in play when with one leg folded
over the other, *Gawain* on my lap, pen clucking

over my notebook, Billy reneges on his conviction:

'I'm hard. But my da's harder.'
Grown-up teeth are a parent's embodiments
the way a factory canteen is for an insect a city;

the way Shelley's calcified heart, resisting fire,

embodied only phenomenon.
'Yea, my hands have been dirty too,'
little Gawain might've said, closing

his hand around his Granny Smith,

miles still from the Knight's hibernation,
his green axe, a correspondence of green.
'To a girdle,' little Gawain might've said, 'to a field of dead,

an interlude of kisses.'

But still Billy's interrogation: 'You ever been inna fight. . . ?'
Coy of my hand succeeding to the squeeze,
my knock-down Nikes redolent of morning dirt.

20:59

Johnny Cope was tasked with keeping prisoners awake,

he tells me, when he served in Afghanistan.

He knows by heart every word of AC/DC's 'Hells Bells'.

'See this?' he yells, raising hell with a piece of pipe on a bin lid,

'Every fifteen fuckin' minutes!'

21:03

'What about that story of "Mushroom Mansions",' I ask Johnny,
'your old flats, yer man "Grem" who lived below you?'

'The screaming trees of my lungs woke me,' he replies,
'and I rang the fire brigade and I knock knock knock knock knocked
the neighbours awake, and I stood with the others
in the early hours of early summer
feeling the inherited heat of yesterday
under my socks, the tarmac infused with sunlight
twice removed, since what we feel is already the past,
all of us in our night clothes, pyjamas, T-shirts,
trackies, flip-flops, bare feet, watching
the flames in the flat below mine creak and crack
and form those evil faces people think they see
in the smoke of disasters, and who's to say
this one was any different since Grem was still inside sleeping
as the fire brigade arrived and began rigging the water,
voluntary Dantes stepping up through the circular
levels to him, unconscious now inside and dreaming
of a light getting brighter and brighter,
or dimmer and dimmer,
and even those christened with youthful names
must bear them into the future, I thought,
Grem who more than once misidentified me
in darkness through acid eyes, a carload arriving
at my door, the head honcho recognizing me from school
from behind his Chelsea scarf and pulling the plug and
disappearing from whatever history remained between us.'

21:07

Just as blood is always trying to escape,
making a break
at the slightest nick,

so it is at 21:04
when Johnny Cope takes it upon
himself to lower the heaviest tool

in the factory
from the heart of the biggest machine,
the chain of the hoisting crane itself

shuddering like a hangman's rope,
onto the only pallet truck available,
far too narrow,

the tool unhooked and finally tipping,
all one ton of which Johnny Cope
takes upon himself to catch,

his crushed wrist and hand
from which, at 21:07,
blood escapes.

21:31

A whiff of burning plastic
in the factory's moon-squares
is a curl of cigarette smoke vanishing
up the chimney of a cold fireplace
on a Saturday afternoon.
What of that budding berry tree
in the graveyard under which
we inhaled and disappeared into
our own lungs and pretended to know.
What of the kids on skateboards,
bunny-hopping kerbs on BMXs,
none of them truly believing.

21:48

Crazy Dale's old Marvel comics
piled in the canteen by the kettle;
late nineteenth-century Alberta
where Thomas Logan is keeping grounds
on the Howlett estate, abusing the drink, his son –
a temper close to superhuman.
A coffee cup stain on the magazine
lends him an angelic air
despite the bottle, despite the hair.

Beyond the canteen the CNC
halfway through its cycle
says the future is as fictional
as the past, and mostly tragedy:
how else could Elizabeth Howlett fall clean
for Thomas Logan,
whose best kept secret was Wolverine.

21:53

Wee Gail's cooking knife,
sharpened on the belt grinder
next to the ancient Tufnol saw
in the machine shop,
would take the tip
off my finger before I'd know it,
it's that sharp, the one I'm using
to dice this cooked chicken breast
and slather it in tamarind sauce.
The edge is honed bright
as the quarter moon.
I imagine working my way down
the finger like you slice a carrot.
I think about this
even when I'm not dicing chicken breast
in the factory canteen.
And the times I think about it
I begin to feel sorry for the hand
to which the finger belongs,
its population of molecules
so used to existing,
so content with their lot,
travelling every day and night
their little valleys and pathways.
On trains, for example,
I think about it. On walks sometimes.

22:11

Ghostly in hi-vis the night guard

gives voice to the hour echoing into
the next and retains no prospect but of trees
and all the dark and chilling dew. Who knows
how he gets from one to two and two to three and on
and though we're all on the same shift

it's true my machine marks time
with each spindle-cutting revolution,
its mundane magic rumouring the future
stacked with Cittiglio's hills and dales,
a dyer hanging his silks from the highest wall.

22:14

How I rehearse each shift
to justify myself to myself,

a cell made up of cells in a cell
whose cells are altered daily

by breathing the factory air, peculiar
with cryptic chemicals drawn

from distant ecosystems,
my circadian rhythm a mirror universe,

O Bay 17, O Cell 42, O spider
keeping company, lapping yourself

on the empty hopper.

22:22

Man is born free, and everywhere he is in supply-chains –

It's a bit like this place,
tethered to the machine
with an option to go hungry, or find another factory
to feel the same in.

It's only in dreams you're truly free
and even then it takes magic;
like that mad one the other night,
where, as a means of escape
from a seventeen-something prison cell

I became a rat,
        and made my way through a crack
which for a second,
in my eyes' lit dark, held the world.

Then, in the way dreams cut between here n there,

I was where the hanged men
        were raised above the shifting earth,

a rat-person in dream-clothing,
watching the condemned

soaring on barley wine,
        as if drunkenness might stand in for death.

I woke before my alarm, lay till it went off, then drove here.

22:30

On the canteen TV humanoid robots work alongside humans in a Japanese factory – 'they are my teammates they are hard workers,' says one of the humans in English subtitles, 'I'm grateful for their hard work.'

Little R2-D2s stack shelves in a Californian grocery store – 'we don't need to give it eyes or a face or a human body,' says one of the designers to the camera, 'for people to relate to it.'

Back in Japan, Professor Ishiguro has built his own double to stand in for him during lectures around the world – 'emotion,' he says to the interviewer, 'is a simple part of being human.'

In some countries plans are in motion to have polling stations manned by robots – 'the social etiquette of movement is fundamentally about trust,' says the narrator, 'the way a vote is a prayer cast into the unknown.'

22:45

Fassbender's 'David' in *Prometheus*
takes Gary Numan as his physical muse
rendering an authentic look for his android,
a vibe not a million miles away
from the lucidly drawn dawn that rises
over the set, the dawn of a foreign planet.
Fassbender has Numan in his ears between takes.
A passage in the script discusses the perils of manufacturing,
the hope that 'David'-kind coming off the conveyor belt
are less and less like humans than humans perceive.
I gleaned all this from a behind-the-scenes vignette,
which I think about as Gary Numan comes on
the factory radio and the timer on my machine beep-
beeps the birth of another plastic aeroplane part.
It puts me in mind of 'David' mouthing ambivalence:
There is nothing in the desert, and no man needs nothing.

23:01

Management returned home
from China promising to improve
conditions for us, the workers,

bearing, like photos they won't develop, 'ideas',
while our lungs glow eerie as Hevea brasiliensis:
not marks the spot but skull and crossbones,

air-bound chemicals heavy with poison
magicked in that rumoured realm of
MAY CAUSE CANCER

23:06

The job card says URGENT!

'cause these parts were due yesterday

and I'm fucked if I can't pay the rent

and here I am with the hour distant,

bound for blame stockpiled on day

shift because this job is urgent

and the night won't make like a tent

and cover my arse so it won't matter what I say

even 'I'm fucked if I can't pay the rent!',

even though the cycle on this job is bent

out of time 'cause the night isn't going to lie

down and this bastarding job is urgent

and these thousand more latches aren't

going to make themselves are they

and I'm fucked if I can't pay the rent,

27

so mould deburr and box like Heaven-sent

mould deburr and box, even pray.

The job card says URGENT!

The important bill's the rent.

23:16

Maybe it's the distance into
        the shift, the energy drawn out

by the ground, but the peacock-tail
        of sparks Billy's grinder conjures

off that curious metal
        is an interstellar dazzler

from that cluster of galaxies dubbed 'peculiar'.

23:20

Wedging my head and shoulders
into the valley of the CNC machine
to shovel a load of Tufnol dirt,
it's the summer of '96 again,

working on the farm
for underage beer,
the summer my favourite calf
became of no more use to the farmer,

its head wedged in a fence, neck laced
in wire – rubies landed like suns
when the bullet left
its eyes staring at nothing.

23:23

Hell as an idea of what work could be:
isn't night meteors as corvettes of love,
or the narcotic beauty of rockets on the news
burning up on re-entry; it's an idea
of what Gary could be (the other Gary),
whistling an entire twelvehour night shift
whatever rhapsody filters through
the fugacious O of his lips –

O for an esplanade,
O for noise-cancelling headphones,
O and that podcast I forgot to download
about the flowering buddleia the kid MacNeice
viewed the sea beyond at Portrush.

23:32

Last week, for fuck's sake,
six hours in a secondhand Sandretto
machine, shaped in brute force
with a steelhead sledge
to hammer free a single bolt
from the moulding tool,
glazed to the elbows in grease,
Jimmy and Jamie,
in the name of 'safety', watching.

23:46

The English call it shavings,
                    the Americans call it chips,
but Here we call it swarf,
                    the metal dust churned up
by the steel cutter creamed in coolant
                    rendering the CNC's guts in glittering
galaxies, which must be exhumed,
                    back n forth between machine cycles,
into bins like pebbled sand into buckets
                    as my little nephew and I did
yesterday morning, whose absence
                    here is everywhere since he said
'Every time I run by
                    I see a lost shell in the middle of my eye.'

00:00

The night is proletarian,
a morgue of ghosts
given the present is a borderline:

if the purpose of existence
is to give meaning
to the lives of others

how does one account for loneliness?

00:02

The relationship between touchscreen and finger
is unbearable, like the Twelfth roadblocks
sprung with fire.
Amid the factory's sad sci-fi
fumes are a cure for hunger,
and the Union flag tangled over the derelict
building is breaking no law.
I think of that summer in Rome,

Vatican City, when having shouldered through
historic vaults we reached the gift shop, a mirage
of white-teethed calendars, a collared Father
for every month, rows of plastic figurines,
where we lingered as a means
of staving off, a little longer, July's unbearable heat.

00:13

By way of example,

last month the shining sea was misleading
despite the day's 23 degrees.
Sometimes it's like you've to be a genius
to get through the hours.

Take this cassette tape booming in the factory
ghetto blaster, possibly the last of its species,
its lazy eye all clockwork orange,
bastardising 'Music for the Funeral of Queen Mary'.

Or the canteen telly showing ossuaries
of keepsakes in carved-out caves
near Jerusalem where no one can agree
it's the Jesus family.

Or the moon just the sun sleeping.
Or the word *you* in a poem,
an act of cowardice.

00:19

The wind at the new steel shutter door
christens the echoes I hear
lost among the machines.
The machines rumble on
and only pause when the programme permits,
when the material won't galvanize:
'They said this was fucking fixed!'

00:21

Old colour rinsed
again & again
reincarnates
briefly, briefly
in new plastic
& scrapped
till surges of blue
through beige
become moments
when something
seemed possible.

00:25

A storm is named for the person
who spotted it. That's myth.
A gust tears the iron sheeting
off the neighbouring unit,
damaging our steel shutter,
a dent so gaping it's the mouth on the cover
of *Music for the Jilted Generation*.
Yer man on Cool FM says it's going to get so severe
that people should stay in and batten down.
The government says employers
should send employees home while they can
but Stevenson complies only by giving us the choice.
All I can think about
is the loose bolt in the courtyard door
below my bedroom window
that bangs and bangs in strong wind.

00:26

Music for the jilted generation,
another piece of my childhood –
Keef Flint no longer here – checked out
over the weekend. 'Serial Thrilla'.

The last photo of him on the internet
shows him setting a personal best
during his local parkrun, smiling
his biggest broadest smile.

He looks like the happiest little boy.

00:27

They filmed the video for 'Firestarter' in a disused
Underground tunnel near Aldwych,
the same tunnel where artworks and artefacts sheltered

from the Blitz. A photo online shows the Elgin Marbles
with the colossal granite head
of Amenhotep III, as the people of London huddle
nearby for the long haul.

A little boy snuggles into his mum.
He looks like a 1940s Keef.
For him that tunnel is the whole world,
the total discrediting of reality,

muscular relics from strange places,
Egyptian pharaohs, his short life.

00:28

I'm thinking about the tunnels here in Kilroot
how the long-range forecast
says no two winters are the same
how the salt mine next door is two hundred million years
and a quarter of a mile beneath the earth
Ireland's only one
– listen the ting n tang of pickaxes
sixty years ago
peace lives above a frenzy of minerals
a salty seam sown all the way to Russia
– and they don't mine under villages
and any land not the government's
is a few gardens
a few feet down
and the guide knows every inch
of the blackness
deeper and deeper
and the monsters there are mechanical
and no longer manufactured –
so long preserved by rarefied air
four hundred metres under World,
Oisin-machines can never again
roll on the Earth –
chomping pillars of salt
sandy-coloured
       – not white

00:29

Once, all around me delusions of understanding,
a diagram of geese hatching ideas
then a scribble of rain.
My workmate's dad sold his own eggs,
that was his hobby.
'Good for hangovers,' he said.
Telling me to be gentle,
he gave me six green goose eggs
bound neatly in a flannel.

01:03

A pigeon has strickened its way
into the factory

and before Joey the pigeon-racing fanatic
snaps its neck in an act of mercy

whatever language pigeon is
the pigeon is speaking death,

its undesperate eye open
and blinking like code:

We're not long for this world
where we once carried messages

and sometimes lost our way
over patchworks of misery.

01:10

Mr. Gramophone the headmaster called me,

in front of everyone, as if my inner
workings were surplus as anxiety
which is the mind in the future:

come back to me.

The boy who spoke in class
whose words were lampblack
grazed by a rigid boar's bristle

'Au clair de la lune'
phonautograms of sound
traced to origins,

come back to me.

The earliest recorded voice has survived,
'By the Light of the Moon'.

01:15

On break I drive to the twenty-four-hour
Tesco's where ignorance is bliss until
I pass the volcano cakes
and I remember my nephew said he's been doing Pompeii
in school, the methods of its preservation.
I wonder for a moment if preservation means perishing in
increments.
The earlier voices of children echo through the aisles.

01:20

The *Daily Mail* thinks it's clever
but the crosswords are always easy,

so we like to ruin them on break
by making up our own.

Imagine Gazza's delight
when he manages to divine the *u* in

f

c u n t

c

k

01:29

When we look up at stars on break
we see only stars behind
the exhaled Milky Way
of Bobby's Golden Virginia,
ways to navigate shift patterns,
nothing seismic or anything approaching
truth; for us stars mean only night shift,
insanity of depth,
the slow individual seconds
during which the dotted starlight
doesn't burn fast enough.

02:02

It's stormy when I flip the blind
to a wayward tarp's interpretive dance.

For most of the night I've imagined
my own POV floating

through the corridors of high school,
slowly, suddenly, observing

each imperfect consolidated rubber mark
on the lino's ordinary sheen.

02:05

Concrete. The misery of concrete
has made my earliest memories grey,
the way a distant cold
forgets me, my fingertips,
and goosebumps infer multitudes.

02:42

The smell of this injection barrel's residue is the year
my mum could sit on her hair

when we watched Evel Knievel jump burnt-out cars
on telly – that's what I remember, those two things,
convinced he was doing his stunts there in Rathcoole.
I don't know why I thought that.

It might've been the month mum bought me his wind-
up toy at our neighbour's jumble sale,
which smelt of nicotine, whose burnt-out mechanism
had long been shot to shit.

02:45

Then there was New Mossley

where no one ever made like the Amish
& raised a barn.
No one ever ripped up
tarmac & planted a garden.
What would be the point;
there was already a square
of grass outside each home
to sit & smoke

Lambert & Butler & capture
the moon in smoke rings.
Conversations were zip-lined
doorstep to doorstep,
every stray cat an imposter.
Granny's house was targeted
three times because my uncle
was on a hit list.

Her wee mutt, Sooty, lived
to be nineteen despite being hit
by three separate cars
on three separate joyrides,
carrying for the rest of his life
scars like drought-land.
The football field's fertilizer
was mostly dog shite,

the stolen cars left an ampersand.

02:59

On the translation boards outside the foreman's office

the oddments of work reach

beyond the English language to
t
r
a
b
a
j
o
in Spanish and
t
r
a
v
a
i
l
in French, both from the Latin
t
r
i
p
a
l
i
u
m
an instrument of torture.

03:07

In the name of fuck!   you'd think the moral order of the universe
depended on the right material   heated to the right
temperature   moulded into the right
part   deburred in the right
way   shipped in the right
manner   fitted in the right
cabin   using the right
tool   in the right
plane   ! am I wrong ?

03:16

Milling machine tables roll out
and in
like slabs in a morgue,
adjusting aluminium parts to
absolute perpendicularity
where parallelism is only one ism
among many:

I just like the jokes
I'm not racist,

and diction is contradiction
according to the contradictionary.

03:18

Which reminds me of the sheep in my dream,
hypothesizing by the year 2099
the ability to tell an android from a human

will carry a success rate of around 3%.
You'll know them by their empathy, it said.
Just as you can tell a racist by the *but.*

Just as you can tell an electric sheep
by our refusal to be counted.

03:19

clang – Dale drops his shifting spanner.

Tragedy ebbs into nothingness at 3 a.m.
when the feet hurt and the head is light.

When the news came out of Pretoria
that Valentine's Day, about the man
who shot his partner through a bathroom door,

I couldn't believe it, but Dale was making jokes;
that's what permanent night shift did to him,
softened murder into dissonance,
opened a space to be filled with humour:

'Maybe he needed a pish
and tried to shoot the lock open.'
He got his phone out and played the *Blade Runner* theme
on his portable Bluetooth speaker,

and I think I know now the horror
Pinocchio felt watching his pal
sprout donkey ears,

then feeling himself begin
to go.

03:20

Every factory has the same lexicon:
cavity, barrel, latch, button, cycle,
part, material, scales, spindle, cutter,
drill, press, tool, pump, machine, nozzle,
bench, bracket, store, shift, spanner,
valve, timer, time, clock, run, break,
program, swarf, dust, coolant, metal,
plastic, purge, which is to say my tongue
moves aimlessly in its mouth.

03:21

In the tesseract of life,

if I could signal

from long ago

before the real was hard

where a prism was only one

among many,

every object of affection

a gömböc,

I'd

speak of equilibrium,

my ear,

so long stopped

with wax, working itself free,

bringing back a piece of the world.

03:29

Thumb-work with the Stanley knife,
when chamfering the plastic edge

of parts gathered from the drill press,
sometimes draws blood,

the burr buckling
heart-shaped off the blade.

04:04

In a reverie brought on by 4 a.m.,
or the machines that bombinate

millennia through their cycles,
I'm back in the Ulster Museum

where you said, 'In this period artists were taught
to discover black via colour.'

Beneath the trees we watched the ways of trees.

'The red is vermilion,
see?'

When you glanced at me
your eyes appeared new

the way naked black was new
in Turner's day.

Without speaking you gave credence
to broken ground.

Do you remember the ways of the trees?
'Soon all the trees in the world will fall.'

04:06

The Bridgeport mill machine
from 1965 pools incontinent
around its base
in the corner of the factory
floor and someone will
eventually have to throw
sawdust on that mess
and clean it up
because parts for that model
can no longer be sourced
so the Bridgeport mill
will have to live forever

04:08

My dog-eared *Gawain*
knows and knows
and keeps knowing
about the coils of existence,
the same question
it has come down to
since the anonymous
time of Anonymous
when a Knight could

pick up his severed

head and ride into
greenness and wait
for the difference one year
or a hundred might make,
only to be asked
when the time comes
'Is this all there is?'
replying
'What else ought there be?'

04:09

Above the factory
whoever walks the narrow path
through the town's unmoored wood

is reminded to wear the night
by the nothing the leaves make
on the branches.

04:18

The last time I flew Flybe
I recognized my own handiwork
in the pristine edge

of the endbay that made up
the seating's lower half,
four hours to Italy –

even on holiday,
even at thirty-five thousand feet,
at five hundred miles an hour,

you can't escape.

04:19

But we were bound for Milan
smack dab in the month of May
and I'd only ever seen the Alps
on television so we looked out
the plane window and there
were the Alps! the actual Alps!
and through plexiglass
it was *kinda* like television but

without the trail of elephants

the suitcases spelling help!

the snowbound bodies

with their backs to the sky

04:33

the 4 a.m. sky
flashes the Technicolor
of Paul Newman's eyes

in *Cat on a Hot
Tin Roof*, the first film to show-
case the blue that would

prove the myth true; like
the myth of the four-ball plant
I made true by fluke,

throwing Luke some shade
on our last Christmas work do.
Bamboozled he was:

'That's the exact same
shot same four-ball plant Newman
in *The Hustler* made!'

05:03

The machine moulding cavity opens

at the end of each cycle
and drops its token, which by the same token
is the material woe

of every open heart's possibility
of another life.
Even the apostles, in this way, divided up

their time and passion.

05:15

There's a time coming and soon
as the moon quests through its phases,
as above little Gawain, who readies
Gryngolet, eager to gallop,
but Gawain only gazes at his coat
and imagines the chapel,
the grievous blow he must receive,
and his man will not go,
not for all the treasure in the ground.

05:20

Near the Winecellar Entry, a bunch of us,
in an empty Belfast, dandering about,
then two horses wandering around.
They look escaped, no bridle, bareback.
We go up to pet them like Clooney
in *Michael Clayton* just before his car blows up.

From nowhere, seemingly, a camel, looking lost
and stressed. We try to calm it, you and me.
It noses our elbows and backs away
like a dog wanting a door opened.
We follow it and keep following it, as it checks back
now and again to be sure we are still there,

to a field on the outskirts of the city
full of mutilated dead and dying cattle.
The camel is wordlessly trying
to get us to help in some way.
I want to cry. You get your phone out for photos.
'What can we do?' I say. 'Nothing,' you reply.

05:29

It was wee Gail's seventieth birthday
last week and she has a special
seat to sit on all shift

and her hands are old at the task,
old at working the tricks that come
with having laboured

in the same place for so long

and she's making light work
of sifting defective ring washers
from those within tolerance and

her bench could be a grand piano,
her patch of floor a stage,
and in another life, it is.

06:01

Them kɾıs' pækəɾs ız dɪeən' ðə tæŋgoh

    Kathy says

Ay'd ə dreem Ay wəz dansən'
ðe aı'r dey –
wohk wı' mə ɑrm roun'
ðə hubi'z næk,
ɑr han'z holdən'.

  the storm's head's

become full with rage

    in the slow dark

quickening with swirls of rubbish from the skip

    a boogaloo of plastic parts.

06:11

Hey Jonathan Swift
what brought you to this parish
all those gigaseconds ago
you were miserable by all accounts
we know we know the prebendal stalls
the Diocese of Connor but ah yes
it was love of course it was
small remote Kilroot far
from the centre of influence
and from your letter we can see
you bowed to love's ultimate cliché
the ultimatum which like love
brings its own agonies.

And I hope it's true you began
A Tale of a Tub here
all those gigaseconds ago
in what's now the Kilroot business and industrial park
where I too am miserable
where your Round House no longer stands
where the devil never caught you in a corner;
they replaced it with a power station
whose round tower is as close
as we'll ever get to a skyscraper
and if one can star the dark
one can satirize it.

And Jonathan Swift
I hope it's true you first thought of Gulliver
on the boat back to England

nursing your broken heart
Cave Hill's gigantic brow nose chin hair
thrown back as the land in its ancient anesthesia
and in the eye of a storm
the distant winds sound like Creation
opening its mouth.

06:15

On the toilet I open my 'notes' app and begin to tap:

as accidents wait
as boredom waits
as illness waits
as comfort waits

06:45

The early morning Mercs are beginning to file in
like copies, incarnations of office management,

gliding through the whirl and gloom of autumn's amber,
the wet tarmac's multiplying light.

07:00

not little Gawain

repenting his misdeeds
crossing himself
over and over
having to sleep
in his armour
manufactured
even then
among sleet and rocks
a moody Christmas
or the dragons
and the wolves
and the trolls
and the bulls
and the bears
and the wild boars
and the ogres

but the decision

that decision he made

07:02

Who could have foreseen
those hatchet-buriers
would land on our shore,
dreams Gawain,
with their distant tongues

and temperament –

'Everything changed,'
his father replies
the night he leaves,
breath-blowing the room
into permanence.

07:16

The storm has reached a perfect volume
    which is to say it's running out of breath
and look the world is still there
    outside and the trees and bushes look
like marathoners at the finish line
    and Kathy does a smiley on the window
and puts her face
    to her own creation.

07:28

that poem about happiness
coming on slowly,

realisation as light drawn
across a factory floor

07:31

who wrote that poem who was it
ah yes that poem about being happy

08:00

Clocking out,
a photo of me drops
into my phone (*whatever happened
to this bow-tied little dreamer*),
three years old or thereabouts
hair all blond and ringlets,
hand in pocket,
heels together
ten-to-two,
and who knows
who I wanted to be
in that past whose future
never came.

In Cittiglio

i.

This is too much, but it happens:
the hill scaffolded with poplars
doing its best impression of a mountain,
the chapel cancelling the heat,
the big dome ensuring the light keeps to itself,
important things happening in the street,
the busker in the alley catching my eye
assuming I might be
jotting down something significant,
the villa's beachball spinning on the pool
slowly as the world,

ii.

the rain respectful, waiting until night to fall
for the shortest skiff,
the smoke from my Toscanello hanging
stubborn, sending its lovely zeppelins
through lengths of hair
to where a single firefly surprises me,
following it through the trees
at the end of the pitch-black garden
to the thousand-strong flashing field,
then gathering together, all of us.
My friends, may our deaths be timely.

Notes

Some of the poems in this sequence, as well as the preceding epigraph, borrow from Jacques Rancière's seminal work, *Proletarian Nights: The Worker's Dream in Nineteenth-Century France* (1989), trans. John Drury.

20:00

The Tina Turner cover of the song 'The Best' (1989) has been adopted by members and supporters of the Ulster Defence Association (UDA). The words are often altered to reflect their ideals.

In 1953, twenty-one-year-old Guy-Ernest Debord wrote 'Ne travaillez jamais' ('Never work') on a wall on the Rue de Seine. The slogan is thought to have been inspired by Arthur Rimbaud's phrase, 'Never will I work', from his collection *A Season in Hell* (1873, republished in 1994 as *A Season in Hell & Other Poems* and translated by Norman Cameron).

21:48

CNC stands for computerized numerical control.

23:01

On particular bags of plastic moulding material there is a stark warning against carcinogenic toxins escaping into unventilated environments, underlined by the maxim MAY CAUSE CANCER above a skull-and-crossbones motif.

23:32

A Sandretto is a plastic injection moulding machine manufactured in Italy.

00:13
"Music for the Funeral of Queen Mary" refers to Wendy Carlos' reimagining of Henry Purcell's 1695 composition which appears as the title track in Stanley Kubrick's film *A Clockwork Orange* (1971).

00:25
Music for the Jilted Generation (1994) is the second studio album by the Prodigy. The cover features a face emblazoned in molten steel, the mouth gaping in distress.

00:26
Keith 'Keef' Flint, lead singer of the Prodigy, died by suicide in March 2019.

00:27
The music video for the song 'Firestarter' (*The Fat of the Land*, 1997) by the Prodigy was filmed in a disused Underground tunnel in London which was used as a bomb shelter during both world wars.

01:10 (i.m. AD)
The earliest known surviving recording of a human voice was made on 9 April 1860, when Édouard-Léon Scott de Martinville recorded someone singing the song 'Au clair de la lune' ('By the Light of the Moon') on his invention, the phonautograph. However, the device was not designed to play back sounds, as Scott de Martinville intended for people to read back the tracings, which he called phonautograms.

Oscar Pistorius was charged with and convicted of shooting and killing his partner, Reeva Steenkamp, on 14 February 2013. He is a former Paralympic champion and was the first-ever double amputee to compete in the Olympic Games.

03:21
A tesseract is a four-dimensional hypercube.

A gömböc is a class of convex three-dimensional homogeneous bodies called mono-monostatic that, when resting on a flat surface, have just one stable and one unstable point of equilibrium.

04:18
An endbay is the piece of plastic covering that makes up the bottom area of an aeroplane aisle seat.

06:01
This poem is written partly in Eejɪt, a phonetic writing system developed by Belfast poet Scott McKendry befitting Belfast vernacular English or 'Belfastwa' (*anglais belfastois*). Eejɪt takes elements from standard English and vernacular ('organic') spelling, the 2015 version of the International Phonetic Alphabet, and other phonetic writing traditions. The Eejɪt alphabet is as follows (approximate IPA referents in square brackets): a [a], ɑ [ɑ], æ [æ], aɪ [ɒ~ɔ], ay [æi], ay̆e [ɒːɪ], b [b], ch {tsh} [tʃ], d [d], ɗ [ɾ], đ [t/ð→d], e [ɛ~ɛə], ee{ė} [i], ėɪ [iə], ey [ɛi], ə [ə], əˉ[əː], ӕ [ɐ~ɜə], f [f], g [g], ɣh [x], h [h], i [ɪ~e], ɪ [ɪ], j [dʒ], k [k], l [l], m [m], n{kn} [n], nk [ŋ], ng [ŋ], oh [o~oʊ], oə [oə], ou [ɜʉ~ɔi], oy [ɔi], p [p], r [ɹ], s [s], sh [ʃ], t [t~ɾ], ƭ [t→ø], ƭh [ð→ø], ťh [θ], th [ð], u [ʌ], u̇ [ɜ], ɩe [ʉ],

v [v], w [w], y [j], z [z], zh [ʒ], ʻ [ʔ], ʼ [ø]. An account of Eejɪt with examples was published in *PN Review* 274, volume 50, no. 2 (November–December 2023).

Eejɪt is used with permission from Scott McKendry. The standard English of the poem reads as: 'Them crisp packets are doing the tango / Kathy says / I'd a dream I was dancing / the other day – / woke with my arm round / the hubby's neck, / our hands holding.'

06:11
Writer Jonathan Swift lived in Kilroot, Carrickfergus, from 1694 to 1696 while prebend in the Diocese of Connor. Rumour has it that he began *A Tale of a Tub* there and that he first had the idea for *Gulliver's Travels* when, on the boat back to England, he observed how Cave Hill's profile resembled the face of a giant gazing at the sky. These rumours have been consigned to local folklore.

07:28–07:31
The poem 'Happiness' was written by Raymond Carver and appeared in his collection *Where Water Comes Together with Other Water* (1985).

Acknowledgements

Thanks are due to the editors of *The Guardian* and *The Poetry Review*, where versions of some of these poems first appeared.

It takes an idea to write a book of poetry, but it takes encouragement, emotional support and practical input from others to see it to fruition. I'd like to thank my mates: Michael Magee, Sacha White, Padraig Regan, Stephen Connolly, Manuela Moser, Ellen Reay, Susannah Dickey, Joey Connolly, Tara McEvoy and Dane Holt, the 'Cittiglio Crew', for many conversations both literary and miscellaneous, and to whom the epilogue of this book is dedicated. I love you all.

To Scott McKendry for his tireless advice, friendship, shoulder to sleep on, and for lending me Eejit. Also, for being a great trans-Atlantic travel buddy. Viva, O'Hanlon's! ('A pitcher of PBR and a house whiskey for $7.00!!??' Oh, gone are the days . . .)

To the Wok-A-Mole Crew: Jake Hawkey, Alanna Offield, Eoin Kelly, Zara Meadows and Matthew McGlinchey for all the bants, and the poetry.

To Rachael Allen, Joley Day, Clare Bogen, Jacques Testard, and all the staff at Fitzcarraldo Editions for believing in my work and for continuing to believe in it. Thanks also to Mensah Demary and Cecilia Flores for first giving this book the green light on the other side of the pond, and to Dan Smetanka, Megan Fishmann, Rachel Fershleiser, Laura Berry and everyone involved at Soft Skull Press for the sterling efforts in putting the book together stateside. I'm truly humbled to have Fitzcarraldo and Soft Skull in my corner.

To my friends, colleagues and teachers at Queen's University Belfast and particularly at the Seamus Heaney Centre for Poetry, where I have learned so much: Nick Laird, Fran Brearton, Leontia Flynn, Glenn Patterson, Dawn Watson, Stephen Sexton, Gail McConnell, Charles Lang, Rachel Brown, Joshua Beatty, Marcella (Prince) McSweeney, Stephen De Búrca, Morgan Leathem, Shannon Kuta Kelly, Ciara McAllister, Bebe Ashley, Charlie McIlwain, Paul Maddern, Tim Loane, Tara West and Garrett Carr.

Thanks to the Arts Council of Northern Ireland for various grants at important times which have helped me enormously, and in particular to Damian Smyth for his advice and mentorship. It has been so important to me.

Thanks to Martin Mooney for important and irreverent chats about all things poetry and the absurdity of this world, and to the respective staff of The Whitecliff Inn and The Marine Bar in Whitehead, County Antrim, where these conversations took place, and where a fair amount of poetry was written in between shifts pulling pints.

Thanks to the Sunday Club crew: Caitriona and Sean, Rosalyn and Rachel, for the interludes and great company, the pints and the nightcaps.

To my parents, Deirdre and Adrian, for their love and support. (Thank you, Dad, for your poet-advice, and for reading drafts of this book).

To my sisters, Charis and Charlotte, for the loving WhatsApp 'Whoo-hoo!'s.

To Finn, our family dog, for being the best listener. We miss you every day. Rest in peace, you beautiful being. This book is dedicated to your memory.

And of course, to my partner, Martienne, for being amazing. *If you're going to San Francisco . . .* x

There's me
at the train station
window leaning

my forehead against
my own reflection
and I'm all

about my dog
and how I think
I love him

the way Holub's Faust
loves the dog
whose pain gives out

the reflected light
of death, *a love*
whose essence

is hopelessness,
just as hopelessness
has its essence

in love, the sacred space
on the back of a dog's
neck where once

his mum
carried him
to safety.

matthew rice was born in Belfast. He holds an MA in poetry from Queen's University Belfast and is currently undertaking a PhD at the Seamus Heaney Centre at Queen's. His debut collection, *The Last Weather Observer*, was published in 2021 to critical acclaim, highly commended for the Forward Prize for Best First Collection, and included in the Arts Council of Northern Ireland's top ten books of the year.